Homes give us shelter from
the weather.

Some homes are in busy cities.

Some homes are in the country.

What Are Homes Made Of?

Some homes are made of stone.

Some homes are made of wood.

Some homes are made of mud.

Some homes are made of grass.

Different Types of Homes

Some homes are small.

Some homes are big.

Some homes are old.

Some homes are new.

Some homes are high up in trees.

Some homes are underground.

Some homes are in caves.

Some homes can move.

Homes are different all over
the world.

Homes
Around the World

Clare Lewis

Heinemann
LIBRARY

Chicago, Illinois

© 2015 Heinemann Library
an imprint of Capstone Global Library, LLC
Chicago, Illinois

To contact Capstone Global Library, please
call 800-747-4992, or visit our web site
www.capstonepub.com

Edited by Joanna Issa, Shelly Lyons, Diyan Leake, and
Helen Cox Cannons
Designed by Cynthia Akiyoshi
Original illustrations © Capstone Global Library Ltd 2014
Picture research by Elizabeth Alexander and
Tracy Cummins
Production by Victoria Fitzgerald
Originated by Capstone Global Library Ltd

Library of Congress Cataloging-in-Publication Data
Lewis, Clare.
  Homes around the world / Clare Lewis.
    pages cm.—(Around the world)
  Includes bibliographical references and index.
  ISBN 978-1-4846-0369-7 (hb)—ISBN 978-1-4846-0376-
5 (pb) 1. Dwellings—Juvenile literature. 2. Dwellings—
Cross-cultural studies—Juvenile literature. I. Title.

GT172.L48 2015
643'.1—dc23   2013040500

Image Credits
Alamy: Images of Africa Photobank, 20, Liquid Light,
17, 22 (bottom left); Getty Images: Abenaa, 10, back
cover, Elisabeth Pollaert Smith, 21, 22 (middle left),
Gerald French, 13, guenterguni, 16, 22 (top right),
Image Source, 15, shayes17, 7, 23 (top); Shutterstock:
Agnieszka Guzowska, 14, antpkr, 3, Chantal de Bruijne,
12, JeniFoto, 4, leolintang, 11, leungchopan, 6, Natali
Glado, 5, 23 (bottom), pgaborphotos, 8, Pitcha Torranin,
1, S.R. Lee Photo Traveller, 24, Tanawat Pontchour,
2, VLADJ55, 19, 22 (bottom right), zebra0209, 18;
SuperStock: Norbert Eisele-Hein/imageBROKER, 9, 22
(top left), Raga Jose Fuste /Prisma, cover

Contents

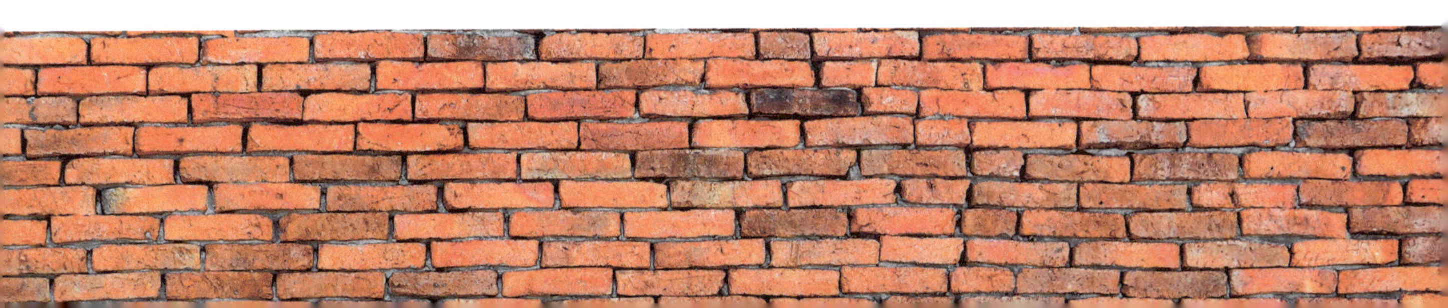

Homes Everywhere

All around the world, people live in homes.

What is your home like?

Map of Homes Around the World

Picture Glossary

country place that is away from towns and cities

shelter place to stay safe

Index

Notes for parents and teachers

Before reading

Ask children about the types of homes they see in their community or neighborhood (houses, apartment buildings, etc.). What types of materials are these homes made of? What other materials do they think homes can be made of? Explain that throughout the world, homes are often made from many different types of materials that are usually available from the area in which the home is built.

After reading

- Turn to page 5 and read the sentence. Ask children if they know what *shelter* means. Do any clues in the sentence help them know? Then turn to the glossary on page 23 and explain that a glossary is a tool that helps explain some of the more difficult words in the book. Find and read the definition for *shelter*.

- Discuss the fact that many of the homes throughout the book are very different, yet there are some things that are similar in most homes. Have children look through the pictures and name the similar features (doors, windows, walls, roof). Have children draw a picture of their home and label these parts.